SEA OTTERS

Sandie Lee Books

Sea Otters

Sea otters are related to weasels. They are in the Mustelidae family and the biggest animal in this category. Other animals in this family include the badgers, wolverines and polecats. This animal is a favorite at many zoos and marine parks because of its playful and whimsical nature. It is thought the otter has been around for about 5 million years. If you think these facts are cool, you "otter" read on to discover more about this interesting animal.

Where in the World?

Did you know sea otters live most of their lives in the water? They can be found in the northern and eastern North Pacific Ocean. These animals live off shore and in kelp beds. They can also be found where there are plenty of places to dive down and to forage for food on the seafloor.

The Body of a Sea Otter

Did you know the body of a sea otter is built for swimming? The sea otter is a heavy animal. Males can weigh up to 99 pounds and females about 73 pounds. It has webbed feet on its back legs and a long tail. Its legs are shorter and its body is long and sleek.

The Sea Otter Fur

Did you know the fur on a sea otter is extremely thick? It has 1 million hairs in 1 square inch of fur! This makes the fur the densest of any other mammal. Its fur has 2 layers; long waterproof guard hairs (hair on top) and a thick short undercoat. This keeps the otter from becoming cold in the water.

What a Sea Otter Eats

Did you know the sea otter hunts for food in the water? This mammal will eat snails, clams, mussels, fish and small organisms found on sea kelp. It forages for food along the ocean floor. It can hold its breath up to 5 minutes. However, most of its dives only last about a minute.

The Sea Otter's Special

Did you know this mammal uses rocks as tools? The sea otter will use its favorite sharp rock to crack open the shells of its prey. It can also move rocks and dig through the mud on the bottom of the sea floor. This is where it finds and picks up clams to eat.

The Sea Otter's "Pouch"

Did you know this animal has a "pouch?" The sea otter has an extra flap of skin under each of its front legs. This acts like a pouch to hold and carry things in. The otter will store its favorite rock, clams and other food that it has foraged, in this extra skin. Once it surfaces, the otter will use its rock to split open and eat its find.

Sea Otters at Rest and

Did you know the sea otter likes to slide? When in zoos or marine exhibits you may notice the otters running and sliding. This is a form of play. In the wild, otters will sleep and rest in a group. This is called, a raft. Sea otters in large groups may hold each other's front paws while floating on their backs.

The Sea Otter as Prey

Did you know sea otters were hunted by man? This species almost became extinct because of overhunting. The sea otter's fur was used to make clothes from. Predators in the wild like sharks, orcas and eagles will also hunt the sea otter, especially the very young, old or injured sea otters.

Sea Otter Talk

Did you know the sea otter can make sounds? A sea otter can scream and whistle. This animal will grunt and coo when it is enjoying a meal. During the mating season, male otters will coo or make a whining, dog-like sound. An angry or frightened otter will sometimes hiss or even snarl.

Mom Sea Otter

Did you know a female sea otter can have young at 3 to 4 years-old? Once pregnant, she will carry her young for around 3 to 4 months. The mother sea otter will give birth to 1 baby otter in the water. Some types of otters will have 2 babies per year.

Baby Sea Otters

Did you know baby sea otter is called, a pup? The pup looks like a fuzzy little ball when it is born. The hair on it is very dense and helps it float. The pup will ride around on its mother's chest and belly when she is floating. It nurses milk from her, which is very high in fat.

Life of a Sea Otter

Did you know sea otters can live to be 15 years-old? Sea otters spend their time foraging for food and floating on their backs. These animals are very smart and social. In addition, they keep the kelp forests healthy. They do this by eating the sea urchin that feed on the kelp.

The Northern Sea Otter

This sea otter can grow up to 5 feet in length and weigh around 100 pounds. Females of this breed are smaller. It can be brown, black or even silver in color. Its front paws have strong toes and the back ones are webbed for swimming. They have small ears and cute faces.

The Giant Sea Otter

This otter is closely related to the sea otter. It is the largest member of this family. It can measure up to 5.6 feet long. It has a sleek body and is active all day long. It eats mostly fish and crabs. It has the shortest hair of all the breeds. It is usually chocolate brown in color.

Quiz

Question 1: What other animals are the sea otter closely related to?

Answer 1: Badgers, wolverines and polecats

Question 2: Where do sea otters like to hang out?

Answer 2: In kelp beds

Question 3: How long can a sea otter hold its breath?

Answer 3: Up to 5 minutes

Question 4: Where is the sea otters "pouch" located?

Answer 4: Under each arm is an extra flap of pouch-like skin

Question 5: What does the sea otter use to open its food with?

Answer 5: A rock

Thank you for checking out another addition from Sandie Lee Books! Make sure to check out Amazon.com for many other great titles.

www.ingramcontent.com/pod-product-compliance
Lightning Source LLC
Chambersburg PA
CBHW050802290526
45792CB00008B/2299

* 9 7 8 1 4 9 5 2 1 1 1 6 4 *